Cover Photo: Normal Gray Zebra Finch cock

Endpapers: Pair of White Zebra Finches

HOWELL
Beginner's guide to
Zebra Finches

David Alderton M.A.

Editor
Dennis Kelsey-Wood

HOWELL BOOK HOUSE Inc.
230 Park Avenue
New York, N.Y. 10169

© 1984 Paradise Press

All rights reserved. No part of this publication may be reproduced, stored in any retrieval system, or transmitted in any form or by any means without the prior permission in writing from the publishers

Library of Congress Cataloging-in-Publication Data

Alderton, David, 1956-
  Howell beginner's guide to zebra finches.

  Bibliography: p. 51
  Summary: A basic guide to the care of zebra finches, covering such aspects as feeding, breeding, showing, and health problems.
    1. Zebra finch—Juvenile literature. [1. Zebra finch. 2. Birds] I. Title. II. Title: Zebra finches.
SF473.Z42A43   1985   636.6'862   85-18138
ISBN 0-87605-949-3

Book design by Routedale Ltd, Liskeard, Cornwall, England
Printed in Hong Kong through Bookbuilders Ltd

Photo Credits:
Front endpaper and P.34 © Panther Photographic International
P.27,30, and 31 © Zebra Finch Society
All other photographs and illustrations © Paradise Press 1984

Contents

1. Introduction	7
2. Accommodation	10
3. Feeding	14
4. Breeding	17
5. Zebra Finch color forms	26
6. Color Breeding	34
7. Showing	38
8. Health Problems	41
9. Classification	44
Appendices	
Aviary Plants and Shrubs	46
Zebra Finch mutations	48
Bibliography and addresses	51
The Zebra Finch at a Glance	52

1. Introduction

The Zebra Finch *(Taeniopygia guttata)* is found over much of Australia, apart from the Cape York Peninsula and other coastal areas in the extreme south-west and east. It does not occur in Tasmania, but island populations are recognized from Sumba and Timor, in the Flores group, to the north of Australia.

Approximately thirteen sub-species have been identified, and these have contributed to the variation in depth of coloration which can be seen in domesticated individuals of the same color. Flocks of wild Zebra Finches are a common sight throughout their range, wherever there is water nearby. They feed almost exclusively on the seeds of wild grasses, and breed with the onset of rainfall in any given area.

The date of their introduction to Europe has been lost, but they were certainly well-known by the end of the nineteenth century. The first description of the species appears to have been made by Vieillot, in about 1805, although it was then thought that they originated in the Moluccas. As aviary birds, Zebras proved prolific breeders and the development of color

Normal Gray cock (left) and hen. Note the orange cheek patch on the cock.

7

mutations, begun during the 1920s, contributed further to the popularity of these finches.

The Zebra Finch Today

These small birds, about 10cm. (4in.) long, are now in fact the most widely-kept species of finch. Their lively demeanor and readiness to reproduce are two of their most obvious attributes, but they also make good exhibition subjects, and the foundation of the Zebra Finch Society in 1952, with the establishment of show standards, encouraged this aspect of keeping Zebras. For the beginner, prices of good quality exhibition stock are much less inflated than in other areas of the Fancy, and it is quite possible to establish a reasonable exhibition stud for a relatively modest outlay.

Zebra Finches are also quite economical birds to keep, as they do not require expensive foodstuffs nor elaborate accommodation. However, they are likely to benefit from the extra feeding period that is made possible by a light left on, for a couple of hours or so, in their quarters during long winter evenings. Zebras are hardy birds, though in cold weather an electric tubular heater in their aviary shelter will keep the temperature above freezing and benefit them accordingly.

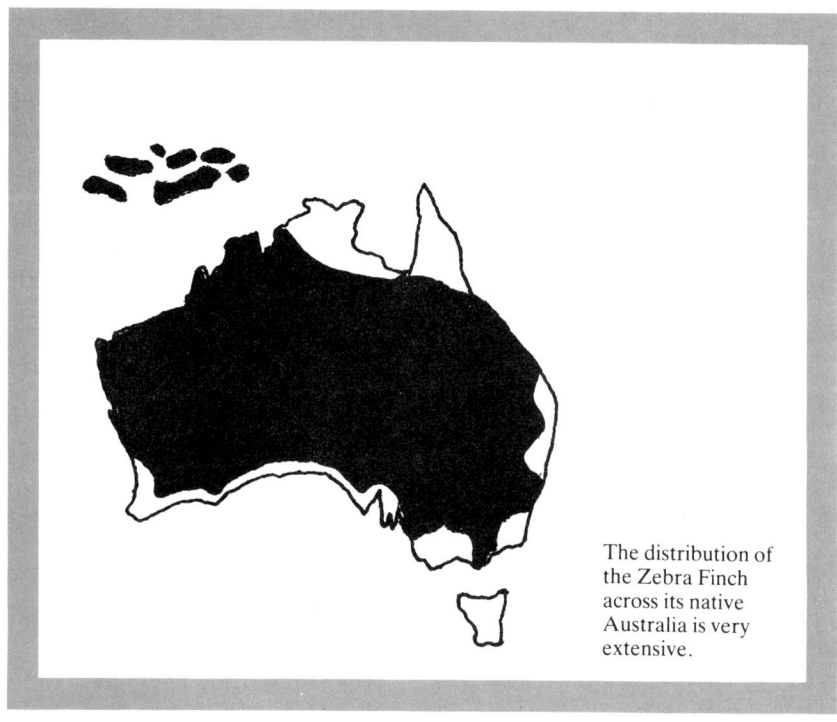

The distribution of the Zebra Finch across its native Australia is very extensive.

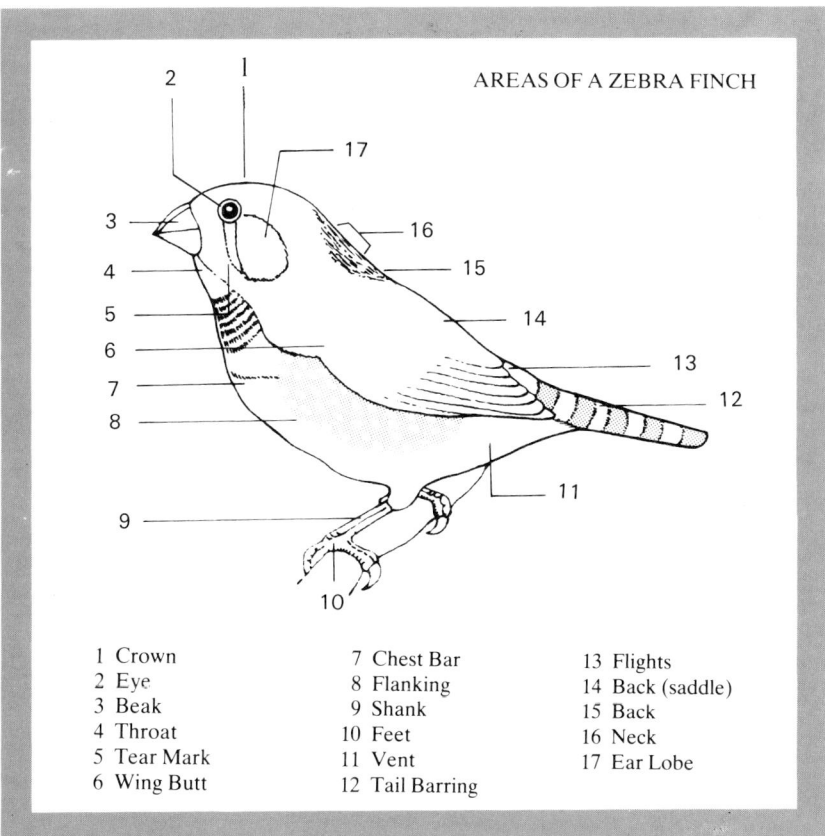

Points About Purchasing Stock

It is probably preferable to purchase young birds rather than older stock, the age of which may be unknown. Although Zebras are mature at as early as three months old, better chicks will result if the adults are not bred from until nine months of age. Healthy youngsters should be alert, moving readily from perch to perch when approached and often uttering their cheeping call.

They can be caught from a stock cage by hand but in an aviary a net, well-padded around the rim, will be essential. They do not bite severely and, to restrain a bird, it can simply be held in the palm of the hand; but, for closer examination, it may be preferable to restrain the head *very gently* between the first two fingers of the hand. It is then possible to feel the chest, which should be plump, with no hollows either side of the breastbone.

2. Accommodation

Zebra Finches do not require elaborate accommodation; a simple aviary comprised of shelter and flight units is sufficient to meet their needs. For those who subsequently wish to breed exhibition Zebra Finches in particular, it is useful to have the aviary incorporated into a larger birdroom, where breeding cages, show cages and seed can be stored.

The Flight

Wired panels, which simply need to be assembled, can be obtained from many firms advertising in avicultural magazines such as *Cage and Aviary Birds* and *American Cage Birds*. Such panels provide a useful short-cut when building an aviary, especially if they are weather-proofed with a suitable preservative; but a jointed framework built to one's own requirements can also be made without too much difficulty.

A Cream cock Zebra Finch

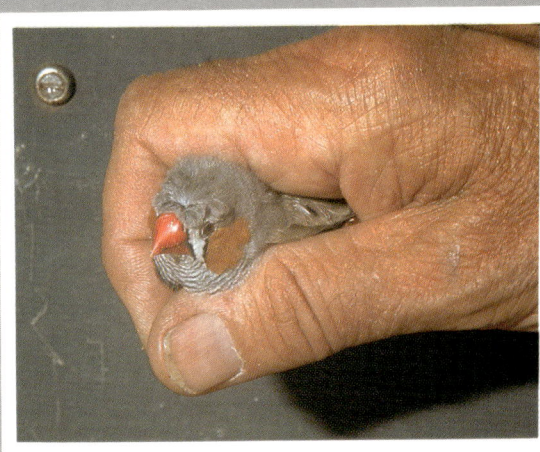

The correct method of holding a bird is shown in these two pictures....

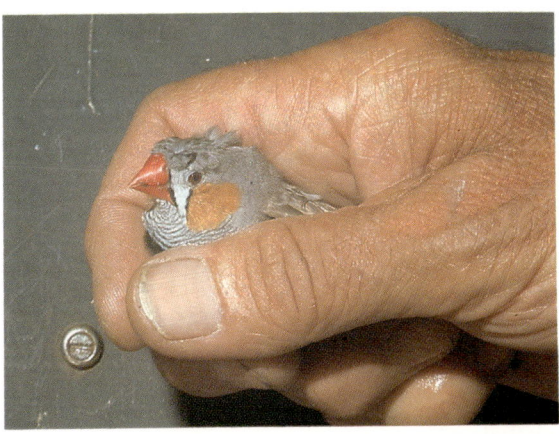

....which also illustrates the Crest variety of Zebra Finch.

Timber of at least 3·75 cm. (1½ in.) square will make a solid framework for the flight. It should be treated with creosote before being assembled into frames, to increase the lifespan of the structure. Providing the woodwork is allowed to dry thoroughly over several weeks before the birds are released into the aviary, this treatment will be quite safe.

The mesh used to cover the flight panels should be 19 gauge (19G) and have maximum dimensions of 2·5 cm. × 1·25 cm. (1 × ½ in.). Netting of this size should also help to keep rodents, and even snakes, out of the aviary. These creatures will certainly create a disturbance and may well eat the eggs, if not the birds themselves. The wire should be attached to the planned inner surfaces of the jointed frames using netting staples and, finally, any exposed and potentially dangerous loose ends should be cut back as far as possible, and then covered with thin battening.

Shelter

A dry, draught-proof shelter attached to the flight will also be required; it must be well-lit to encourage the birds to roost therein when the weather is bad. A door, leading from the shelter into the flight, should be included in the design as well as an entrance hole located near the roof for the birds to use. Their entry can be facilitated by providing a simple landing platform on either side of the entrance hole. A shelter 90cm. square (3ft) is suitable to match a flight 270cm. (9ft) in length.

Foundations

The whole structure should be mounted on a firm base, constructed using blocks or bricks sunk into the ground around the perimeter. Apart from providing additional stability, with the aviary bolted to its base, secure foundations should also serve to keep out rodents and foxes which may otherwise tunnel in, with fatal consequences.

Ideally, the floor of the flight should be of concrete – which is much easier to clean satisfactorily than is grass – sloping away from the shelter to allow for adequate drainage in wet weather. The shelter will also require a solid floor, which can be covered with old newspapers to catch the birds' droppings and seed husks. The floor-covering will probably need to be changed once or twice weekly.

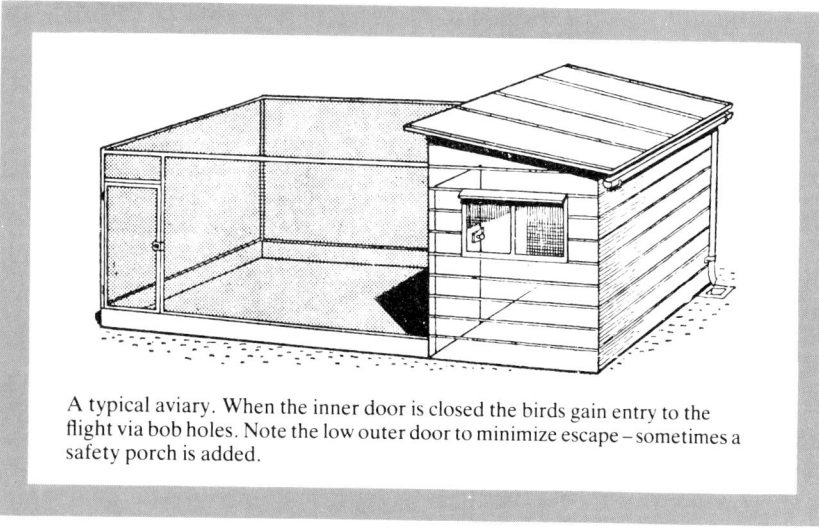

A typical aviary. When the inner door is closed the birds gain entry to the flight via bob holes. Note the low outer door to minimize escape – sometimes a safety porch is added.

Perches

Zebra Finches can develop foot sores if the perches in the enclosure are unsuitable, and supple branches are preferable to hard dowelling. Some variety in the diameter of the perches is also to be recommended, but they should never be so thick that the birds cannot grip them adequately, nor so thin that the birds' front toes curl right round to the back. Perches can be constructed in the shape of a 'T', and fixed in the floor, or be suspended by means of wire loops attached firmly to the aviary framework. They must always run across the flight, rather than down its length, so the maximum possible flying space is easily accessible to the birds. In addition, perches should not overhang feeding utensils, because these are likely to be soiled by droppings from above.

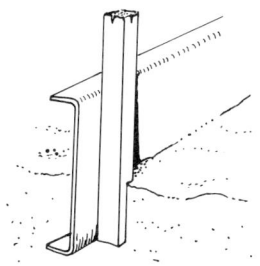

Sheet metal nailed to the uprights and turned over, above and below ground, is recommended for making an aviary mouse-proof.

There are many trees and plants which can be utilized as a source of perches. The fresh or dried stalks of some herbaceous plants, such as Golden-Rod *(Solidago* spp.*)* are useful, especially in cages, and can be changed as necessary. However, it is important that none of the wood used for perches should recently have been sprayed with chemicals. Branches cut from yew trees, lilac and laburnum may prove poisonous and should be avoided. Perches are also sometimes soiled by wild birds, so all branches ought to be washed before use.

Roofing

The roof of the flight nearest to the shelter should be covered with translucent plastic sheeting, for perhaps 180cm. (6ft), and a similar distance on the sides. This will enable birds to sit outside with some degree of protection when the weather is bad.

The shelter itself can conveniently be roofed with marine plywood, with all cracks being filled with a suitable water-proofing material, and tarred over, before heavy-duty roofing felt is applied. This should overlap for several inches down the sides of the shelter. As a final precaution, to ensure that the interior remains dry, guttering should be attached along the back of the sloping roof, to carry rainwater away from the aviary.

3. Feeding

Zebra Finches are not difficult birds to feed, and they will thrive if given a mixture of seeds and some green-food daily. Millet of various types, along with plain canary-seed, form the basis of most foreign-finch mixtures which are ideal for Zebra Finches. An adequate mix can also be prepared easily by giving a half dish of panicum millet, topped up with equal proportions of other millets, especially Plate Yellow and Japanese, as well as a part of plain canary-seed. Red (Dakota) Millet and Pearl White, which is relatively large, are generally less popular ingredients in a mixture. Apart from these cereal seeds, a small amount of niger is also beneficial, particularly just prior to the breeding season, as it is thought to help protect against egg-binding. Niger does, however, contain relatively high levels of fat, so should be fed sparingly.

In addition to loose seed, millet sprays are extremely popular with Zebra Finches. These can be offered in a dry state, or soaked as described below. They are, in fact, seed heads containing panicum millet. In the light of recent American findings though, it may be preferable always to soak them first. Along the stems of these millet sprays are minute sharp projections which can be swallowed by the birds, and are then found in the throat, and even the crop, at post-mortem. They could also penetrate the feet, and may lead to infections developing here. However, the actual harm caused by these tiny barbs is at present unclear, but soaking apparently renders them innocuous, as they too are softened.

Soaked Feed

When seed is immersed in water, it is encouraged to sprout and the chemical changes which would naturally accompany germination take place, altering its feeding value. Vitamin levels increase, as do those of protein, while the seed itself is also rendered more digestible. Soaked seed is, therefore, commonly fed when there are chicks in the nest, and to birds recovering from illness. It can, however, be offered daily throughout the year, and contributes useful variation to the diet.

The required quantity will need to be left to soak for a day in a warm environment, and then washed thoroughly in a sieve. Only small amounts

SOME EDIBLE GREEN FOODS.

should be prepared at any one time, because molds soon develop on such seed, and any that remains uneaten has to be discarded at the end of the day. Feeding containers, separate from those used for dry seed, are necessary and open pots are often utilized for perishable foodstuffs. It is also possible to purchase plastic bases to fit jam jars and these, when inverted, act as a reservoir for dry seed. They have the added advantage that seed is not fouled unnecessarily by the birds' droppings.

Seed should only be purchased from a reliable source, preferably in sealed bags which can be transferred to bins, thus keeping it dry and away from rodents. Their excrement can transmit serious diseases, such as salmonellosis, to the birds if it is allowed to contaminate seed.

Greenfood

Greenstuff, such as fresh-cut lettuce, chickweed or spinach-beet leaves, is popular with most Zebra Finches. Spinach has the additional advantage that, when planted in a garden, a supply is generally available throughout the year, even during the winter. Seeding grasses of various types, including cultivated bird-seed, are also greedily taken by the vast majority of birds. Sweet apple and grated carrot also prove acceptable to some individuals.

Whenever gathering fresh foods for the birds, care should be taken to ensure that it has not obviously been fouled by other animals, or contaminated by chemical sprays. Roadside verges are especially hazardous collecting areas because, apart from the risk of spraying, the lead levels of the vegetation are generally higher as a result of vehicle fumes. This chemical can accumulate in the body until toxic levels are reached.

Grit and Cuttlefish

Both are important sources of essential minerals, with grit also serving to assist with the digestion of food, and they should always be available to the birds. Cuttlefish bone is a major source of calcium, required particularly during the breeding season for sound egg-shells and a healthy skeletal structure in the chicks. These bones are often found washed up on beaches, especially at certain times of the year. Provided that they are not contaminated with tar, cuttlefish bones can be used safely, after being thoroughly cleaned, then soaked for a week with daily changes of water, before finally being washed off thoroughly and left to dry. Pieces should be scraped off the soft side for the birds, in case they have difficulty gnawing the bone directly.

Additional Food Supplements

A range of rearing foods, and even softbill mixtures, prove acceptable to Zebra Finches and, because of their relatively high protein levels, are particularly valuable during the breeding season. Various tonics can also be beneficial, especially during the molt, provided that they are used as directed. Harmful side-effects may well result from the overuse of this latter group of products.

4. Breeding

Breeding cages can be built in a variety of combinations, apart from single units. For example, double cages with removable centre partitions are useful because they can be converted simply to form larger flight cages, for young stock or birds prior to a show. Foreign-finch fronts are ideal for all breeding cages, having narrower bars than those produced for budgerigars, so the birds should not accidentally get stuck between them. These fronts, available from many larger pet stores or by mail-order from avicultural suppliers, are available in an assortment of sizes, and it is preferable to choose a relatively large one, so that the cage itself will be quite roomy.

A basic box design will be needed, with the front comprising the fourth side. Thin plywood is perhaps the most durable material for making the cage, but hardboard is a possible alternative, with its glossy surface forming the interior of the structure. Sufficient space, such as 2·5cm. (1in.) must be allowed for a removable, sliding tray which will facilitate cleaning of the cage. If an external nest-box is to be used, then holes corresponding to the

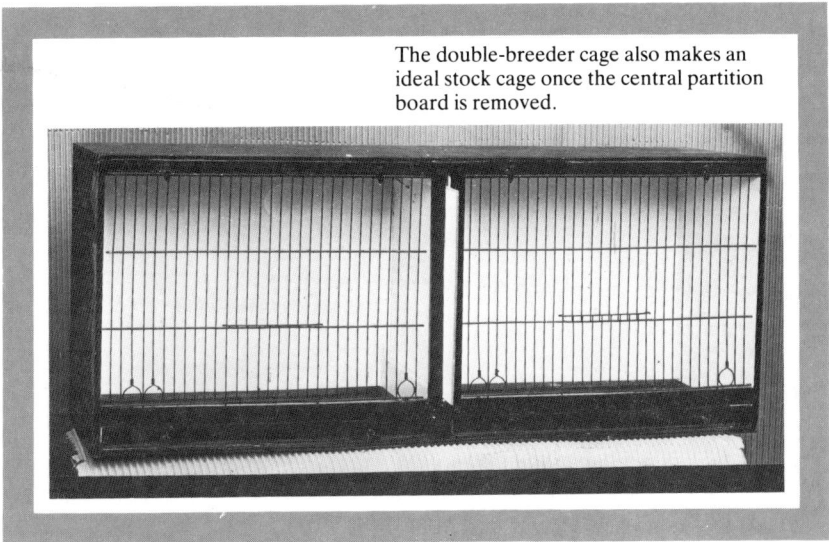

The double-breeder cage also makes an ideal stock cage once the central partition board is removed.

nest-box entry point, as well as to its perch, will need to be cut relatively high up at one end. Small brackets are often used to attach the box firmly to the cage, and yet ensure that it can again easily be removed and washed out thoroughly when the breeding season finishes.

The whole of the interior of the cage will benefit from having a coat of suitable light emulsion paint, which will not be harmful to the birds once it has dried thoroughly. The perches can then be put in position, running across the cage from front to back. It is important that these are fixed firmly in position because, otherwise, the birds may not be able to mate successfully.

This pair of Zebra Finches were quite happy to lay their clutch of six eggs in a cardboard nest-box.

The wicker nest-basket is ideal for most finches including this pair of Normal Gray Zebra Finches.

Nesting Sites

Boxes are most commonly used, although wicker finch nesting-baskets will yield good results as well. The major advantage of a nest-box, however, is that inspection of the eggs and chicks is much more straightforward, thus creating less of a disturbance to the adult birds. Zebra Finches generally make good parents, but interference should always be kept to the minimum necessary, or a pair may start to neglect or even abandon their chicks.

A simple box, in the form of a cube with dimensions of 12·5cm. (5in.) made out of thin plywood, and complete with a securely hinged roof, is ideal. The birds' entrance to the box can be by a circular hole, or a rectangular panel, cut out from the front, with a perch sited below the opening to give easy access. If boxes of this design are used, they will need to be hung outside a breeding cage, so that the roof can be opened when necessary.

Zebra Finches will build a loose nest and, to encourage them, the box should be partially filled with canary nesting material, available from many pet stores. Some breeders use hay without having problems, but it can be dusty and may contain fungal spores which, particularly under damp conditions, are likely to be extremely hazardous to the birds.

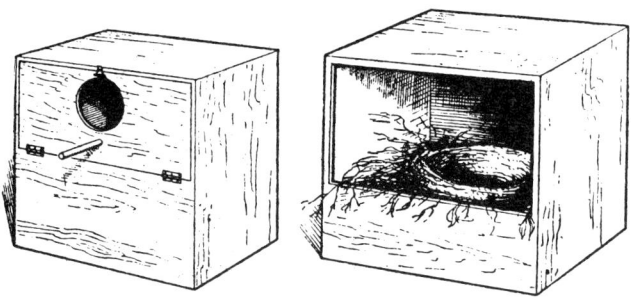

Additional material should be teased out and stuck between the cage bars, where it is less likely to become soiled. The initial nest can then be added to by the birds themselves but, once the hen has laid, no further material should be given, as her mate especially may continue building and obscure the eggs so that they become chilled. This problem can also arise if the birds have access to loose green-food in large quantities and, as a deterrent, it should be tied together in bundles before feeding, or chopped up into small pieces.

Breeding Zebra Finches in Colonies

Squabbling is a relatively common occurrence when Zebra Finches are being bred in this way, but there are various precautions which should serve to lessen the risk of losses. However, these need to be taken in advance of the breeding season.

In the first instance, there should be no birds without mates in the aviary, nor should they be overcrowded. A minimum number of two boxes per pair will need to be provided, fixed up under cover. All nest-boxes should ideally be positioned at the same height, eliminating, from the outset, possible squabbling for the highest nesting site.

Breeding

When in breeding condition, cocks sing and display boldly to their intended mates, chasing off rivals; whereas hens are often seen carrying nesting material in their beaks. Although Zebra Finches can breed throughout the year, it is preferable to commence breeding operations in the late spring. During warmer weather, egg-binding is less likely to become a problem, and there is reduced risk of the eggs or chicks becoming chilled when the adults leave the nest. Prior to laying, the hen will spend longer periods of time in the nest-box, and most consume increased amounts of cuttlefish bone, which is vital for sound egg-shells.

The eggs are white in color, and the clutch varies in size from about three to ten in number, although between four and six is more usual. Incubation may not start in earnest until the second egg is laid, so two chicks may hatch together in the first instance. Both members of the pair take turns at incubating the eggs and, subsequently, feeding the chicks.

A pair of Penguin Zebra Finches settle down for the night – both share the incubation duties.

A pair of Chestnut-flanked White Zebra Finch cocks.

Rearing

The chicks should begin to emerge approximately twelve days after the first egg appeared, bearing in mind that the adult birds may not have started incubating in earnest immediately after laying. On emerging from the egg, the chicks are tiny and unfeathered, with their eyes firmly sealed.

Most pairs do not mind careful inspection of their nests, providing this is carried out sensibly. Once the chicks have hatched, a quick daily inspection is rarely resented, especially if green-food or a soaked millet spray is used to distract the adults' attention. It is preferable not to disturb a sitting bird, however, if this can be avoided. The presence of a favored food item may well suffice to draw the parent off the nest. Rearing foods should then be given in increasing quantities as the chicks develop.

Fledging

The youngsters grow rapidly and usually fledge between fifteen and eighteen days. Once the chicks are feeding independently, they should be transferred to a separate cage, usually about one week to ten days after leaving the nest. This is especially important when the chicks are being reared in breeding cages, as they may be keener to return to the nest-box, disturbing the adults in the process. Most pairs will lay again after one round of chicks, and may well attack their early youngsters if they are still in the immediate vicinity.

Ringing

There are two types of ring, or band, referred to as 'closed' and 'split'. The former serves to guarantee the age of the bird concerned, because it can only be applied while the chicks are in the nest. It is probably easiest for the inexperienced to apply closed rings when the chicks are just starting to develop feathers. The supplier of the rings will normally give details of how to apply them, along with a suitable tool, but it is probably wise to get advice from or, better still, watch an experienced fancier ring his stock. Celluloid split rings can be put on to the leg at any age, and are especially useful for identification purposes as they are produced in a wide range of colors. Potential exhibition stock should, however, be close-rung as explained in the chapter on showing.

Problems During the Breeding Season

Failure of the eggs to hatch can occur for two main reasons, either they were not fertilized or the embryos died in the shell. In the former case, mating was unsuccessful and, when the birds are being bred in cages, they should be shut out of the nest-box for a week, in the hope that this will encourage them to mate successfully. If clear eggs again result, the pair concerned should be split up and given new partners. Lack of fertility is not a widespread problem in Zebra Finches, however, particularly among those being kept in aviaries.

Penguin cock and Fawn hen Zebra Finches.

Instances where the embryo died can be spotted by examining the unhatched egg in a good light, as it will be opaque rather than relatively clear. Low humidity and mineral deficiencies may be implicated in such cases, with the former cause most commonly seen in birds breeding in indoor surroundings. Daily spraying around the box, and the use of a suitable tonic may, therefore, be useful.

Eggs will also fail to hatch if they are not incubated properly and, again, pairs nesting in cages are more easily disturbed. A piece of translucent plastic, clipped over part of the cage front nearest the nest-box, gives nervous birds a greater sense of security, whilst not reducing the light inside the cage too dramatically.

On rare occasions, it may be necessary to foster out chicks and, fortunately, the vast majority of pairs will readily accept this additional burden, providing their chicks are of a compatible age. Eggs can also be moved satisfactorily, as long as there is no large discrepancy between the dates of laying because, otherwise, the youngest chicks, even if they hatch, are unlikely to survive in competition with much older nest mates.

If one member of a pair dies when breeding, the surviving bird may well continue feeding the chicks, but the burden should be lessened by fostering if this is possible. Under these circumstances, it is generally preferable to move the eggs, but some individuals will cope with hatching and rearing chicks on their own.

A Zebra hen (left) gathers soft-food, which she retains until it is at body temperature, before feeding the fledgling which goes through its display routine in order to attract her attention.

5. Zebra Finch Color Forms

For ease of the reader's possible future reference, the color forms are listed alphabetically.

Albino Zebra Finches

This mutation occurred in Australia, but such birds are still relatively rare in Britain, although they have been bred there since the latter part of the 1950s. They are immediately distinguishable from Whites by their characteristic red eye color.

Chestnut-flanked White Zebra Finches

Chestnut-flanked Whites were first observed in Queensland, Australia, amongst flocks comprised of normal Grays. Some hens were caught and, from these birds, the present day strains arose. Australian fanciers still refer to these birds as 'Marked Whites' but, elsewhere, the obvious feature of the cock's chestnut flanks led to the adoption of this term for the mutation. This avoids confusion, as it serves to separate such birds from ordinary Whites, for example, which merely show signs of flecking.

In Europe, the Chestnut-flanked White is commonly known as the Marmoset, and these birds seem to differ slightly from British strains, with their black markings often being more prominent. The British Chestnut-flanked White (often abbreviated to CFW) always has a pale skin, whereas some of the continental birds are dark-skinned, with this distinction being especially obvious when the chicks are unfeathered.

For exhibition purposes, it is quite permissible for Chestnut-flanked Whites to have flecked heads. Indeed, selectively trying to remove these markings over several generations results in a general deterioration of the other characteristic markings in both sexes.

Cream Zebra Finches

This color form results when diluting mutations are combined with Fawn, to produce Cream offspring. The original pairings in the case of the Dominant character revolved around Dominant Silver × Fawn crosses. It is important

A pair of Chestnut-flanked Whites
and a pair of Fawns.

to avoid using either light or dark Fawns when aiming to produce Creams, because the contrast between body color and markings will be adversely affected in one way or another. Even-colored individuals are to be desired, and those which show a patchy depth of coloration, as with Silvers, should be discarded from the breeding program.

The Recessive form of the Cream mutation can be bred using Recessive Silver × Fawn pairings, but various breeders have produced birds of this type from other matings. Cyril Rogers, who has done a great deal to further interest in these delightful finches, reported the appearance of a Recessive Cream cock from Gray parents. This pair had over a dozen youngsters, but only the one Cream chick was bred. When this cock was subsequently mated with two Gray hens, only Gray youngsters resulted and, in turn, these birds were paired together to produce Recessive Cream chicks of both sexes. No Silvers were produced at any stage by this strain, which was surprising.

Crested Zebra Finches

The first Crested Zebra Finches were noted by Herman Heinzel, in Spain, during the late 1960s, and this mutation has also occurred elsewhere in Europe. Such birds can be bred in any color, while the crest itself should ideally be even, and of the full-circular type seen in budgerigars.

Crested Zebras remain uncommon, at present, while on the show bench, as with crested mutants in other species, a combination of Crested and Crest-bred in the appropriate color may be acceptable, instead of a pair of Crested birds. When breeding crests, the significance of the lethal factor, discussed in the genetics chapter, must not be overlooked.

Fawn Zebra Finches

Fawn Zebra Finches arose spontaneously in the wild, and were again developed as a color-form in Australia, initially around Adelaide, from 1927 onwards. The two original hens were trapped near a fire, being drawn there by the low temperatures experienced at night in the outback. Their offspring were not well-marked, and became known as 'Smokies'.

When birds of this mutation first appeared in Britain, the lighter examples were initially called Fawns, with darker birds being referred to as Cinnamons. There is still a noticeable difference in the depth of coloration between individuals, but all are now known as Fawns. It is a good idea to view such birds outside, in natural light, to obtain a well-matched pair, which is a vital consideration for the show bench. By using Fawn parents, strains can be built up very successfully, providing the adults are evenly-colored in the first instance, apart from being of good type. Chicks have brownish beaks on leaving the nest.

Gray Zebra Finches

The Gray is the wild form, commonly seen throughout much of Australia.

As aviary birds, Gray Zebras are still a popular variety in their own right, apart from contributing to the development of the many mutations now available. This has left its mark, however, and led to the deterioration of some strains of Grays. In such birds, white markings may be evident on the head, extending down to the back in some cases while, most significantly, the wings often appear brownish, with individual feathers having a lighter edging.

Thus, it is often difficult to obtain pure homozygous Grays, because the majority are likely to be split for another color but, for the serious breeder, it is not difficult to build up a strain of genuine Grays. Some individuals are, however, darker than others, and this should be borne in mind when selecting pairs for exhibition purposes. The birds must, as with all colors, be matched closely for this characteristic. Youngsters fledge with blackish beaks, as in the case of other dark varieties, and these begin to change within a fortnight of leaving the nest.

Penguin Zebra Finches

It would appear that Penguins were bred in Australia by the late 1940s, and L. Raymaekers of Brussels introduced the mutation to European fanciers in 1949, with examples reaching Britain in about 1952. There, they were initially referred to as Silverwing or White-bellied Zebra Finches.

As with Pieds, only Fawn and Gray Penguins are bred seriously, as these show adequate contrast compared to other varieties. Penguins are not popular today, however, and quality stock remains in very short supply. It is hard to match first year birds for color because, as they mature, cocks get the dark lacing on the wings earlier than hens, and this then becomes more prominent with successive molts.

Pied Zebra Finches

Birds of this type can be bred in combination with any given color, but Gray and Fawn Pieds are most commonly seen as the contrast in these cases is more distinctive. The first strain of Pieds was built up in Denmark, beginning about 1935 although, prior to this, occasional reports had been made of birds with odd white feathers.

The production of good quality exhibition Pieds is difficult, because the show standard for birds of this type is very exacting. Nevertheless, the breeding of Pieds for pleasure is also quite absorbing, seeing the varying patterns of markings which can result. In this case, the distribution of markings can be ascertained from hatching onwards. It is quite likely that a Dominant Pied mutation will occur in the Zebra Finch, as has already taken place in budgerigars and lovebirds.

Silver Zebra Finches

There are two recognized forms of the Silver mutation. The Dominant form

A Silver pair of Zebra Finches and a Cream cock.

A Fawn Pied cock and a pair of Normal Gray Zebra Finches.

appeared in Australian aviaries, and was being bred in Europe by the late 1940s. The Recessive Silver mutation, which is genetically distinct, with a differing mode of inheritance, was Danish in origin. Zebra Finches of this form are generally darker in coloration than the corresponding Dominant individuals.

These mutations exert a diluting effect on an existing color, in this case Gray. The Recessive form is relatively scarce at present, probably because it is easier to breed Dominant Silvers. Nevertheless, a gradual improvement in Recessive Silvers should result from pairings with Gray/Recessive Silver birds over subsequent generations.

White Zebra Finches

The White form of Zebra Finch was the first mutation to be firmly established; although, towards the end of the nineteenth century, Russ records mutants which were subsequently lost. Whites were bred initially by A. J. Woods in Sydney, Australia, during 1921. This is a separate mutation from the Chestnut-flanked White, and should not be confused with it.

There is now a trend towards producing White 'Pieds', rather than genuine Whites, for exhibition purposes. Such birds are, in fact, pure white and, perhaps surprisingly, lack the traces of dark feathering which mar the appearance of many true Whites. They are also of better type, which is an important consideration in exhibition birds of this variety. Continual crossings with Pieds will produce a proportion of Whites of this type but, if possible, only top-quality Pieds should be used for this purpose. Fawns are also popular with some breeders to achieve a similar effect; such flecking as occurs is less prominent in the offspring, being brownish rather than gray.

A pair of these birds gave the Zebra Finch Fancy a major boost back in 1972, when a pair shown by Len Harris took the supreme award for best exhibit in the show at the National Exhibition, London. Without the characteristic difference in markings between cocks and hens evident in Whites, it may be difficult on occasions to select pairs, as a few hens have relatively dark beaks. When exhibiting, however, it is important that birds should show a clear distinction in beak coloration. White chicks, in fact, fledge with pale, yellowish beaks, but these soon change to the characteristic red color.

Yellow-beaked Zebra Finches

The only distinguishing feature between these and other Zebra Finches is that the beak is yellowish rather than red. The body coloration is virtually unaffected, but may be marginally paler in some yellow-beaked birds. Indeed, the yellow color itself can be quite variable in its depth and probably can be improved by selective breeding. At present there are no separate classes for Zebra Finches of this type, and they are shown alongside red-beaked birds of the same color in the appropriate class.

Other Mutations

Several other mutations are in the process of being established in various countries of the world. Black-fronted Zebra Finches, for example, are becoming increasingly common in Australia, and in cock birds of this type, the barring on the chest is replaced by a broad black band. A similar autosomal recessive mutation arose in Germany during 1968, where it is known as *Schwarzbrust* or Black-breasted form. In this case, split cocks can actually be recognized, because they have more prominent ear lobes, plus a broader breast bar, while the tear and flank markings are less conspicuous.

Some strains of this type have been afflicted with liver problems, but individuals are now being bred in Britain. Barry Debling was probably one of the earliest breeders there, having obtained a pair of these birds during 1977, which proved to be poor parents. When Black-breasted Zebras are paired to Whites, a separate color form, referred to as *Schimmel* is produced. Such birds are predominantly white with grayish flecked upperparts extending to the back, and cocks possess a degree of barring on the chest.

Light-backed Zebras have also been developed on the European continent, where they are known as *Helbrücken*. Cyril Rogers has been one of the breeders pioneering the establishment of this mutation in Britain, having obtained his initial stock during 1975. Such birds were predominantly pale gray but, unlike Silvers, had the usual depth of black coloration in their tear and tail markings, as well as in the chest barring of cocks. The ancestry of these early imports is thought to have been derived from Light-back × Continental CFW stock. Subsequently, the body color of Light-backs bred from pairings to Grays or other Light-backs has proved to be somewhat darker.

Various other varieties have also been reported, such as Lead-cheeks and Pastel Browns, while in America, a strain known as Florida Zebras, which appear to resemble Penguin CFWs, is currently being developed. A Grizzled mutation, where the body coloration is broken by white spots, appeared in Australia during the late 1960s, and some of these birds are now being bred in Britain. A strain of Black Zebra Finches has yet to be produced, although odd individuals have been reported from time to time. Doubtless new mutations and color forms will appear over the course of subsequent years.

6. Color Breeding

Although there are now many mutations of the Zebra Finch, the mode of inheritance will fit into one of four simple groupings based on the work of the early geneticist Gregor Mendel. Structures, referred to as genes, control all features of an individual, including color, and occur on chromosomes. These chromosomes are paired, so that there are two genes for each characteristic, located on opposing chromosomes.

Autosomal Recessive Mutations

As the number of offspring produced increases, so the chances of a mutant occurring are correspondingly higher. In the majority of cases, however, the natural coloration remains dominant, and the mutation is referred to as a recessive. If one member of a pair of genes becomes mutated, in this example for Pied, then the bird will still appear like a normal Gray, but carries the Pied gene in its genetic make-up. This mutant gene can later be expressed if the Zebra Finch is paired either with a similar 'split' or a Pied. There are in fact five possible basic pairings for mutations of this type:

1. Pied × Gray → 100% Gray/Pied.
2. Pied × Gray/Pied → 50% Pied plus 50% Gray/Pied.
3. Pied × Pied → 100% Pied.
4. Gray/Pied × Gray → 50% Gray/Pied plus 50% Gray.
5. Gray/Pied × Gray/Pied → 50% Gray/Pied plus 25% Pied plus 25% Gray.

The oblique line indicates that the bird is split for the second color (or character), with the dominant feature preceding it. Such birds, with differing genes, are also referred to as heterozygous, while those which are, in effect, pure may be called homozygous.

Sex-linked Recessive Mutations

Such mutations are confined exclusively to the pair of sex chromosomes, which can be distinguished between the sexes, while the remaining chromosomes are known collectively as autosomes. In the case of the cock, both members of the pair of sex chromosomes are of the same length, whereas

A beautiful study of the White Zebra Finch.

hens have one of these (often denoted as 'Y') shorter than the other (known as 'Z' or 'X'). Therefore, it is not possible for a hen to be split for a mutation which occurs on the unpaired portion of the chromosome, because there is no corresponding portion for a gene on the opposing chromosome to be present, and thus suppress it. Hens must be either Fawn or Gray, and they cannot be Gray/Fawn as can cocks. Expected results for such pairings are:

1. Gray cock × Fawn hen → 50% Gray/Fawn cocks plus Gray hens.

2. Gray/Fawn cock × Gray hen → 25% Gray cocks plus 25% Gray/Fawn cocks plus 25% Gray hens plus 25% Fawn hens.

35

3. Gray/Fawn cock × Fawn hen → 25% Gray/Fawn cocks plus 25% Fawn cocks plus 25% Gray hens plus 25% Fawn hens.
4. Fawn cock × Gray hen → 50% Gray/Fawn cocks plus 50% Fawn hens.
5. Fawn cock × Fawn hen → 50% Fawn cocks plus 50% Fawn hens.

In individual cases, the chicks produced will probably not conform to the expected results, simply because these are based on expectancies from a large number of pairings. As more chicks are produced from an individual pair, the closer expected and actual results will correlate, assuming, of course, that the genotypes for the birds are known accurately. It cannot be assumed, for example, that a supposedly split Fawn cock does not, in fact, carry the mutant gene if no Fawn offspring emerge in just one nest of chicks. The presence of a single Fawn chick will, however, be sufficient to confirm that its father is heterozygous, if its mother is Gray.

Dominant Mutations

There are, however, several mutations which are dominant to Gray, so that a reverse situation to the autosomal recessive mutations exists. In this case, the mutant birds are known as single or double (s.f. and d.f. respectively), depending on whether one or both genes are affected. The Dominant Silver is shown below as an example of these pairings:

1. Dominant Silver (s.f.) × Gray → 50% Dominant Silver (s.f.) plus 50% Gray.
2. Dominant Silver (d.f.) × Gray → 100% Dominant Silver (s.f.)
3. Dominant Silver (s.f.) × Dominant Silver (s.f.) → 50% Dominant Silver (s.f.) plus 25% Dominant Silver (d.f.) plus 25% Gray.
4. Dominant Silver (s.f.) × Dominant Silver (d.f.) → 50% Dominant Silver (s.f.) plus 50% Dominant Silver (d.f.).
5. Dominant Silver (d.f.) × Dominant Silver (d.f.) → 100% dominant Silver (d.f.).

Once again, it is not possible to distinguish between the single and double factor birds by visual means. If Grays result from the pairing of a Dominant Silver with a Gray, however, then the former must be a single factor bird.

Although the Crested mutation is dominant, it should be noted that such birds are not paired together. As with crests in other species, there is thought to be a lethal factor involved, which makes double factor birds non-viable, so that they die in the egg. Therefore, Crested Zebras should always be mated with plain-head stock, and the resulting youngsters will be of both types.

It is possible to calculate the offspring resulting from any pairing, simply by breaking down the characteristics of the parents, and arranging these in the form of a square at right angles to each other. The mating of a Dominant Silver with a Pied is used as the starting point for the example given below. The Silver's genetic make-up is abbreviated to SSPP and, being dominant, it is written in capitals, distinguishing it from the Pied which is recessive in character and referred to as sspp. This yields offspring which are all Dominant Silver (s.f.)/Pied (SsPp). When such birds are paired together, the following results can be expected:

Parent\Parent	SP	Sp	sP	sp	
Gametes	SP	Sp	sP	sp	
SP	SSPP Silver (d.f.)	SSPp Silver (d.f.)/Pied	SsPP Silver (s.f.)	SsPp Silver (s.f.)/Pied	P O T E N T I A L G E N E S
Sp	SSPp Silver (d.f.)/Pied	SSpp Silver (d.f.) Pied	SsPp Silver (s.f.)/Pied	Sspp Silver (s.f.) Pied	
sP	sSPP Silver (s.f.)	sSPp Silver (s.f.)/Pied	ssPP Gray	ssPp Gray/Pied	
sp	sSpP Silver (s.f.)/Pied	sSpp Silver (s.f.) Pied	sspP Gray/Pied	sspp Gray Pied	
	POTENTIAL GENES				

It is not possible to distinguish between single and double factor birds, or split Pied individuals without trial pairings.

7. Showing

Many newcomers to Zebra Finch breeding soon progress to showing their birds and, if this is the intention, then suitable foundation stock should be obtained from a recognized exhibitor who will, in most cases, also offer useful advice. There may be a considerable difference between aviary and exhibition birds, particularly in the case of Pieds, for example, where the markings are crucial.

Zebra Finch Societies

The intending exhibitor should join the nearest local area society, which will lead to contact with other breeders in the vicinity, as well as their national Zebra Finch Society. In Great Britain this society came into existence during 1952, when ten fanciers met at the Crown Hotel in Birmingham. Thirty years later, the organization now has a membership in excess of one thousand four hundred people, and seven area societies have been established. The Club Show can command an entry of over four hundred pairs of birds, and all members receive a handbook and three newsletters annually. Similar societies are now well-established in other countries, including Australia and America as well as on the European continent.

Some varieties are more popular in certain areas than in others, with Penguins, for example, being seen less often at Scottish events. Indeed, most exhibitors begin to specialize in breeding certain colors or types for the show bench, rather than keeping a haphazard selection. Therefore, good pedigree records are essential, based on the birds' ring numbers. If it is intended to enter current-year Zebras in the special breeders' classes, then these must be close-rung with the exhibitor's personal rings issued by the Zebra Finch Society. These are numbered sequentially, and details can thus be entered in a stud book.

Show Entries

A schedule listing all classes, together with an entry form, should be obtained from the Show Secretary, as early as possible before the event, and then carefully completed. If there is any doubt over any pair, the birds should be entered and can subsequently be withdrawn, but late entries after the published closing date are never accepted.

Front and profile views of the Normal Gray Zebra Finch.

Show cages today are largely standardized, with the Zebra Finch Society having laid down requirements for the British design. Second-hand cages with two doors for drinkers should not be purchased, however, because the standard was changed, giving only one access for a drinker, and the older models are now no longer acceptable when exhibiting for Society awards. No personal identification nor the cage maker's name is allowed on cages, and any which infringe this rule will be disqualified as being 'marked'.

Cages should have a white interior, with a glossy black front and exterior. The paintwork must never appear chipped or dirty, as presentation of the exhibits is also significant to the judge. The cage contains two perches which run from the back to the front.

Exhibition Birds

Zebra Finches are always shown as matched pairs of the same color. The major faults of the various varieties are listed elsewhere, and these may differ somewhat according to the particular variety. Pieds, for example, make more demanding exhibition subjects than Albinos. Nevertheless, irrespective of color, several fundamental points must be met before any pairs will be seriously considered for an award.

Both members of the pair must be in perfect condition, with immaculate plumage; this rules out molting birds and those with deformities such as lost claws. The birds should correspond as closely as possible in terms of physical appearance, being selected both on grounds of size and depth of coloration. Individual faults, including drooping wings and tail, or flat head will severely prejudice the chances of the other bird.

Zebra Finches also need to show themselves well, remaining perched while the judge assesses them. This can only be achieved with training, preferably from an early age, getting the birds used to the confines of the show cage, and then to movement close at hand. A pencil waved around at the front of the cage will serve as a substitute for a judging stick, to which the finches will soon become accustomed. If carrying boxes are to be used, then the birds should also be familiarized with this environment before a show.

A STANDARD ZEBRA FINCH SHOW CAGE.

Gaining Experience

The novice exhibitor should try to attend as many shows as possible, and acting as steward to a judge can be a particularly valuable experience. The most consistent winners usually prove to be those breeders who have a clear insight into their stock, its weaknesses and requirements. Regular success on the show bench can only be built up over a period of time, rather than being achieved instantaneously. The interest and enjoyment of meeting others with a similar hobby is, for many exhibitors, as significant as winning and, indeed, this aspect of showing should never be overlooked.

8. Health Problems

There are various diseases to which Zebra Finches are susceptible, but if kept under suitable conditions they rarely fall ill and may live for seven years or more. If an individual is thought to be unwell, it should be transferred to a warm environment, about 30°C (85°F), and veterinary advice sought without delay. A hospital cage with a heater, or an infra-red lamp, can be used to maintain this temperature. Following recovery, the bird should be reacclimatized gradually, before being released back to its companions.

A sick Zebra Finch will often appear dull and fluffed-up, as well as losing its appetite. It may well sit on, or close to, a food pot, picking at the contents with little determination and, if left, will soon become huddled on the floor of the cage or aviary. Weight loss, termed 'going light', can be detected by distinct hollows either side of the breastbone in individuals which have been unwell for a while. If a bacterial infection is responsible for the illness, it should respond well to the correct antibiotic therapy, providing the prescribed dose and instructions for use are closely adhered to. Viral infections, however, cannot be treated successfully with antibiotics.

Cuts and Bleeding

Bleeding will usually occur if a claw has been trimmed too short and, for this reason, the blood supply which is visible as a thin, darker red streak, must always be clearly located before nipping off the end of an overgrown nail. The beak also receives a partial blood supply, and the risk of hemorrhage is again present if it is not cut back carefully. Some comparison with a normal beak is useful before actually carrying out the procedure, for which a strong pair of scissors or bone clippers should be used. In cases where bleeding is a problem, the application of a styptic pencil or a cold solution of potash alum to the wound, should stem the blood loss.

Egg-Binding

This is a potentially fatal disorder which requires rapid treatment. It results from an egg becoming lodged in part of the reproductive tract; thus, it is only seen in hens which have been showing signs of breeding behavior. A shortage of calcium, chilling, and immaturity of the bird concerned are all possible factors involved in the development of this condition. In cases of calcium deficiency, the egg may only have a soft rubbery shell.

Hens suffering from egg-binding initially appear fluffed-up and unsteady when perched. A close watch should, therefore, be kept for these symptoms, particularly in birds laying for the first time, during a sudden spell of cold weather.

When egg-binding is suspected, the bird should be kept in a temperature of about 30°C (85°F). This alone, in some cases, is sufficient to ensure that the egg is passed successfully. If there is no improvement, however, within several hours, it will need to be removed by other means, either very carefully by hand using an adequate lubricant such as olive oil or, perhaps, by an injection of calcium borogluconate undertaken by a vet. In a bird the size of a Zebra Finch, however, this condition may well prove fatal. Birds which do recover should not be allowed to breed again for the remainder of the season, and a check should be made to ensure that adequate cuttlefish bone is available to all stock.

Enteritis and Diarrhea

Gut disorders are not common in Zebra Finches that are kept in clean conditions, but sour egg-food, for example, is an ideal environment for bacterial multiplication, and birds can become affected if they eat such food. Seed soiled with the excrement of rodents is another potentially hazardous source of infection for birds.

When a Zebra Finch is thought to be suffering from a digestive disturbance, it should be isolated and placed in a warm environment, with water available within easy reach. An appropriate antibiotic often effects a cure, providing it is given early in the course of the infection. The aviary and feeding vessels will also need to be cleaned thoroughly.

Eye Disorders

These are often first noticed as a reddening and swelling of the eye, so that it becomes closed. If both eyes are affected, this could be a sign of a generalized infection. Antibiotic ophthalmic ointments applied several times daily are usually of help in curing eye infections.

Feather Plucking

This is a relatively common vice, particularly in birds that are overcrowded. Other factors, such as Red Mite, may also be implicated in some cases. Plucked Zebra Finches have bald areas, often on and around the head, where the feathers have been removed by another bird. An improvement in their surroundings, and possibly also their diet, should help to overcome the problem. Some birds become plucked at the start of the breeding season, especially if there is a shortage of nesting material, but the lost feathers are soon replaced.

Parasites

Red Mite *(Dermanyssus gallinae)* lurk in dark areas, such as nest-boxes, coming out to feed on the bird's blood. This can cause anemia, especially in young Zebra Finches, and an overall loss of condition. All mites, and lice as well, are easily destroyed by means of a safe aerosol spray, while the birds' quarters must also be washed with a similar preparation.

Respiratory Problems

As with enteritis, there are potentially many common causes for breathing disorders, some of which will respond well to antibiotic treatment. In the event of an outbreak of respiratory disease, veterinary advice should be sought without delay.

A pair of Pied Zebra Finches.

9. Classification

The purpose of classification is to divide the entire animal kingdom into a series of groups (called ranks) based on the similarities of features found within animals. The higher the group, the more general its characteristics. Thus, the highest rank is that of Kingdom, embracing all living forms, and these are divided into many phyla, each containing many members, all of which share common features. Phyla are divided into classes, these into orders and so on, until one reaches the individual animal or species, by which time the animals resemble each other in all but the very smallest details.

Over the years, and with the advances in knowledge of the various animals, it becomes continually necessary to revise the classification, especially of the lower ranks. For this reason, you will see differences in the classifications given by various authors, which represent the extent of information on that particular bird or group of birds at that point in time. In order to overcome possible confusion in the nomenclature of animals, it is internationally agreed that Latin be used.

The classification used in this book is based on that proposed by Peters in *Check List of Birds of the World* (1937). All birds belong to the class Aves, with the order Passeriformes embracing all finch-like birds as well as many softbills.

The lowest two ranks, the genus and the species, when used together, identify the members of a single interbreeding group or species. Within a species, there may be one of more races which differ sufficiently to warrant their being given the rank of sub-species, and they are denoted by an extra name appearing after the species name. It is customary to write the scientific name in italics, or the genus if used on its own, but not for any rank above the genus. This latter group always commences with a capital letter and the species name (the trivial) starts with a lower-case letter. The name which often appears after the specific name is that of the person who first classified it and, should the bird have changed from its original genus to a new one, then the person's name is placed in parenthesis. If the name is followed by a date, this signifies the date when first classified. Where a trivial name is repeated, this is called the nominate race and indicates that it was the first of that species to be classified; it is, therefore, an example of the 'type', though, not necessarily typical of the species.

The following shows the classification of the Zebra Finch:
Class: Aves
Order: Passeriformes
Family: Estrildidae
Sub-family: Estrildinae
Genus: *Taeniopygia*
Species: *T. guttata*
Sub-species: *T. guttata guttata* (Vieillot)
             T. guttata castanotis (Vieillot)
(Thirteen sub-species in total are recognized.)

Aviary Plants and Shrubs

Common and (Scientific) Names	Type	Remarks
Blackberry (*Rubus fruticosus*)	Berried Plants	The variety *procerus* sprouts very large berries.
Dog Rose (*Rosa canina*)		Has scarlet hips and attractive flowers.
Elderberry (*Sambucus nigra*)		Black berries in the Autumn; will grow almost anywhere.
Hawthorn (*Crataegus monogyna*)		Plant close together to make screen, ideal nesting sites.
Mountain Ash or Rowan Tree (*Pyrus aucuparia*)		Red berries in clusters, around August.
Snowberry (*Symphoricarpus albus*)		Many birds find this a desirable plant.
(*Cotoneaster salicifolia*)	Evergreen Bushes	Grows to about 1·53m. (5 ft). White flowers precede red fruit.
(*Cupressus erecta*) *viridis*)		Beautiful tree, ideal roosting of hardy birds.
Fire Thorn (*Pyracantha coccinea*)		Red berries in Autumn. Attracts insects so helps dietary variation.
Holly (*Ilex aquifolium*)		If plentiful supply of berries desired, then both sexes of the plant must be grown together.
Oregan Grape (*Mahonia aquifolium*)		Very hardy shrub that survives most ravages or soils. Height over 1·53m. (5 ft).
(*Rhododendron*)		Will outgrow all but largest aviaries, *Caucasicum* is much smaller. Do not plant in limey soil.

(Clematis montana)	Perennial Climbing Plants	Quick growing. White flowers late Spring. *Jackmanii* type sports purple flowers.
Honeysuckle *(Lonicera henryi)*		Red flowers in June. An evergreen ideal for aviary posts or such.
Jasmine *(Jasmine officinale)*		Summer or Winter varieties produce white or yellow flowers in January–February.
Annual Hop *(Humulus japonicus)*	Annual Climbing Plants	Sow at the bottom of posts for effective masking.
Canary Creeper *(Tropaeolum peregrinum)*		Ideal for growing up netting. 3m. (10 ft) in a season. Yellow flowers.
(Cucurbita)		Gourds make interesting additions. Hang from aviary wire or nets.
Runner Bean *(Phaseolus multiflorus)*		Grown on the netting it gives good cover to finches.
(Delphinium)	Perennial Plants	Many birds enjoy the seeds of this plant.
(Linum narbonese)		Linseed is produced from this genus, so is a welcome addition for its seeds.
Michaelmas Daisy or Aster		Many varieties, 1·53m. (5 ft), lavender blue flowers in October.
Paeony *(Paeonia officinalis)*		Many sweet scented varieties. Leave undisturbed when planted.
Solomon's Seal *(Polyganatum officinale)*		Very hardy – plant in the grass of an aviary.
Sunflower *(Helianthus multiflorus)*		Very vigorous in growth, can be planted anywhere.
Tree Mallow *(Lavatera olbia)*		Deep red flowers grow up the stems in July and August. 1·53m. (5 ft).
Valerian *(Centranthus ruber)*		Very hardy, can be planted anywhere. Roots are said to have a deterrent effect on Rats.

The Zebra Finch and its established mutations – descriptions, inheritance of characteristics and exhibition faults.

Color	Cock	Hen	Mode of Inheritance	Exhibition Faults
Albino	As for the White, but Albinos have bright red eyes.	As above.	Sex-linked Recessive.	None is recognized.
Chestnut-flanked White	White plumage replacing gray seen in the Normal. Breast barring reduced to black band as far as possible. Tear markings and ear coverts retained, along with tail barring. Ear coverts orange rather than chestnut.	As above.	Sex-linked Recessive.	Birds tend to be cream rather than white. Black markings often rather pale. Hens may show signs of chest markings.
Dominant Cream	Cream on head, back and wings, variable in depth of coloration. Tear markings gray, chest barring brown to grayish-brown. Black seen in the tail of the Normal also replaced by pale gray.	As above.	Dominant.	As above; poor contrast between body coloration and markings also a fault.
Recessive Cream	Resembles the Dominant form but generally darker.	As above.	Autosomal Recessive.	As above.
Crested	Can be bred in whole range of colors. Crest should be flat, positioned at centre of the head, with feathers of equal length. Crest-bred form indistinguishable from another individual bred from non-crested parents.	As for the appropriate variety.	Dominant with a lethal factor.	As above, plus crests often uneven in size and shape.
Fawn	Resemble Normals, but gray plumage replaced by fawn of variable depth of coloration.	Resemble Gray hens, but fawn in color.	Sex-linked Recessive.	Flank markings poor. Chest barring unbalanced or divided in cocks, should not be present in hens. Paler coloration in some individuals so they are not well-matched with their partners. Tear markings washed out.

Gray (Normal)	Head and neck gray becoming browner on the wings. Chestnut ear coverts separated by black 'tear' markings from region of white extending from around the bottom of the eye up to the beak, merging with characteristic zebra-like barring on the chest, becoming jet black with white underparts. Flanks reddish-brown, with white spots. Rump white, tail barred black and white. Eyes dark brownish-red, legs reddish and beak bright red.	Lacks the chestnut patches below the eyes, the barring on the chest and the flank markings. Beak paler than that of a cock.	—	Any signs of barring in hens, uneven bar in cocks. Flank markings too small. Poor coloration, and tear markings.
Penguin	Can be bred in a whole range of colors, but Gray and Fawn forms most distinctive. Total loss of barring on throat and chest, so white plumage from lower beak to under surface of tail. Body coloration also diluted. Lacing on back and wings seen from second molt.	As above, with white cheek patches	Autosomal Recessive.	Any signs of barring in birds of either sex. Absence of lacing effect.
Pied	Gray or another color replaced in part by white areas to give equal amounts of both, excluding the underparts, on the same individual. Body markings should be broken.	Matches the cock for color; beak usually paler.	Autosomal Recessive.	Absence, or unbroken appearance, of cock's markings. Unbalanced proportion of areas of white plumage. Any chest barring in hens.
Dominant Silver	Silvery-gray plumage replacing areas of gray and black seen in the Normal. Cheek patches much paler, as are the flank markings.	Matches the cock for color; beak paler.	Dominant	Upperparts may show signs of fawn and cream coloration. Indistinctly-marked flanks. Faded tear marks. Any chest barrings in hens.
Recessive Silver	Resemble the Dominant variety, but generally darker, with cheek patches more orange than cream.	As above.	Autosomal Recessive.	As above.
White	Completely white plumage. Eyes remain dark, however.	As for cock but generally has lighter-colored beak.	Autosomal Recessive	Any signs of dark feathering in birds of either sex.
Yellow-beaked	Can be bred in association with all colors. Beak yellow rather than red.	As with red-beaked varieties, the yellow in the case of a hen is paler.	Autosomal Recessive	As for the appropriate color form.

Normal Gray Zebra Finch cock.

Normal Gray Pied cock.

Bibliography & Addresses

The following books may be useful for further reading:

Alderton, D.	*Guide to Cage Birds*, Saiga Publishing, Hindhead
	Looking After Cage Birds, Ward Lock, London
Arnall, L. & Keymer, I. F.	*Bird Diseases*, Balliere Tindall, London
Bates, H. & Busenbark, H.	*Finches and Softbilled Birds*, T.F.H., Neptune, N.J.
Gallerstein, G. A., D. V. M.	*Bird Owner's Home Health and Care Handbook* Howell Book House, New York, N. Y.
Immelman, C.	*Australian Finches*, Angus and Robertson, Melbourne
Rogers, C. H.	*Encyclopaedia of Cage and Aviary Birds*, Pelham Books, London
	Zebra Finches, K & R Books, Edlington, Lincs
Rutgers, A. & Norris, K. A.	*Encyclopaedia of Aviculture Vol. III*, Blandford Press, Poole
Vriends, Dr. M. M.	*Breeding Cage and Aviary Birds*, New York, N. Y.

The Zebra Finch at a Glance

Distribution	Australia, apart from the Cape York Peninsula and some coastal areas. Also islands in the Flores group.
Scientific name	*Taeniopygia guttata.*
Family	Estrildidae.
Longevity	Up to about 8 years.
Size	10 cm. (4 in.).
Average Breeding age	9 months–6 years.
Size of clutch	3–10 eggs.
Average number of eggs	4–6.
Sexually dimorphic	Hens in all cases have paler beaks. Other more distinctive differences in some cases.
Do both parents incubate?	Yes.
Nestbox dimensions	12·5 cm. (5 in.) cube.
Number of mutations	10+.
Upper breeding age	Generally lower in hens than cocks. Fertility falls gradually in older birds.
Characteristic of young	Different beak coloration to that of adults.
Young leave nest	15–18 days.
Weaning age	25–28 days.

Endpapers: Excellent group study containing cock and hen Normal, Fawn, and Cream Zebra Finches.